PLEASE PRAY
FOR THE INTENTIONS OF CLAN WESTON
ESP. FOR CALEB AND KEVIN
AND THE SOULS OF MIKE, RAFAEL, AND JEAN

HOW TO USE THIS BOOK

If you are looking to start memorizing the Rosary in Latin this book is for you. Each prayer is broken down into 5 levels that progressively remove more words from the lines and onto the right hand facing page. By the last level all the words are removed, only blanks remain, and the entire prayer is jumbled on the facing page. Fill in each blank on each level until you are writing the full prayer yourself. For an extra challenge cover each facing page with a piece of paper before seeing the word bank and try to recite the missing passages from memory.

By saying the Rosary in Latin you join yourself to the great chain of Saints that have been devoted to these prayers, and to Our Lady, going all the way back to Saint Dominic. By praying in Latin you may pray exactly as they did.

Latin itself is one of the greatest treasures of human history, and although it is the language of the Church and of Rome it is more than just an artifact of a time or place. Indeed, it transcends history if only for one reason. Above the cross was nailed the title "Jesus the Nazarene, King Of The Jews", in Hebrew, in Greek, and in Latin. We revere the Holy Land because our Saviour walked there - yet how often do we think to revere the very languages that hung above the cross?

By memorizing these prayers you may take that ancient connection to the Saints, to the Blessed Mother, and to Christ on Calvary Himself with you throughout every day of your life. Use the reflection page at the end of each section to meditate upon these prayers and revisit your thoughts on them later.

Most importantly take notes, fill in the blanks, and write whatever you need so that you know these prayers so well that you don't need this book anymore. Once memorized they go with you, through joy and hardship, 'til we all meet again.

Best of luck!

NARONAPUBLISHING.COM
BOOKS, ART, AND GUIDES

- Omnia Ad Jesum Per Mariam -
Libelli nostri gaudium doctrinamque veritatis speramus tibi dare.

Brendanus, Dux

The Most Holy Rosary: Crown Of Roses Eternal

Few devotions in this world match the fervor of devotion to the Holy Rosary, and almost none are so well known even to non Catholics.

Indeed, for Catholics who are seeking to pray the Rosary in Latin there is no introduction necessary. The Rosary may already be a part of your daily prayers in another language, or you may be searching to at last memorize the words that you already read so often. So many learned Saints and popes have recommended the Rosary through history that it seems folly to try to add anything new here. But for some a brief explanation of the Rosary and its history may be helpful.

The Rosary prayers are simple enough. We repeat the greeting of the Archangel Gabriel to Mary "Hail Mary, full of Grace!"150 times and in between we pray the words Our Savior Himself gave to us "Our Father, who art in Heaven". Those 150 Hail Marys and 15 Our Fathers are accompanied by a handful of others, the Glory Be, Fatima Prayer, Salve Regina, and

the Apostle's Creed to form a devotion that encompasses all the tenets of the faith and most of the prayers that will be known to all the laity.

Accompanying each decade, the name for every set of 10 Hail Marys, are meditations that invite us to view the events of Our Lord's life as his mother, the Blessed Virgin Mary, did. These are the 'Mysteries' and they are divided by the types of events that they depict: Joyful, Sorrowful, Glorious, and Luminous.

All combined the Rosary as we know it today is not merely a simple repetition of prayers but a journey through the life of Jesus Christ. We put ourselves "in the scene" with the Holy Family, with the Apostles, and with Christ himself all the way from the Annunciation to the Resurrection, Ascension, and crowning of Mary in Heaven.

While various types of prayer beads have existed throughout history, the form of the Rosary itself, the cord with beads and crucifix, is also unique. But how? Other types of prayer cords do exist: in 11th century England we find bead strings for praying "Paternosters", Our Fathers, and to this day in Greece and the Levant you can still find Orthodox men reciting the Jesus prayer along a frayed prayer rope as they walk or clacking the beads of their komboloi, "worry beads", sitting at a cafe. Other religions, too, have prayer ropes and beads of their own.

What, then, makes the Rosary special?

Tradition holds that the Rosary as we know it came not from a gradual development of the bead prayers of previous eras, but from the Virgin Mary herself. In 1214 Saint Dominic withdrew into a forest near Toulouse in order to pray, seeing the difficulty in converting the Albigensian heretics. After three days of intense prayer Mary appeared to Saint Dominic, founder of the great Dominican order, and presented him a string of beads, saying "if you want to reach these hardened souls and win them over to God, preach my Psalter.", that is, the Rosary. Saint Louis de Monfort repeats this from Blessed Alan de La Roche.

Ever since then the Rosary has been especially beloved by the Dominicans and spread widely across the whole world.

As Catholics we believe that the Rosary is a powerful prayer, indeed Our Lady implores us repeatedly in her apparitions to pray the Rosary daily. It has been associated with many miracles, not least of which is the victory of the Catholic forces over the Ottomans at the battle of Lepanto, now commemorated on October 7th as the feast of Our Lady of The Rosary.

This volume focuses on committing the prayers of the Rosary to memory through repetition and writing. Each prayer has five exercises for memorizing, an English translation, and a page to write your own reflections.

Because memorization takes practice we've also included a QR code at the end of this book where you can download these worksheets for free to print out on your own

If, as Saint Padre Pio said, "the Rosary is the weapon for these times" then memorize these prayers to never go unarmed in the great spiritual battle of our era.

Pray that Mary, Our Lady of Victory, may help us win souls for her Beloved Son, Jesus, in Whom the greatest victory has already been won.

MEMORIZE
THE HOLY ROSARY

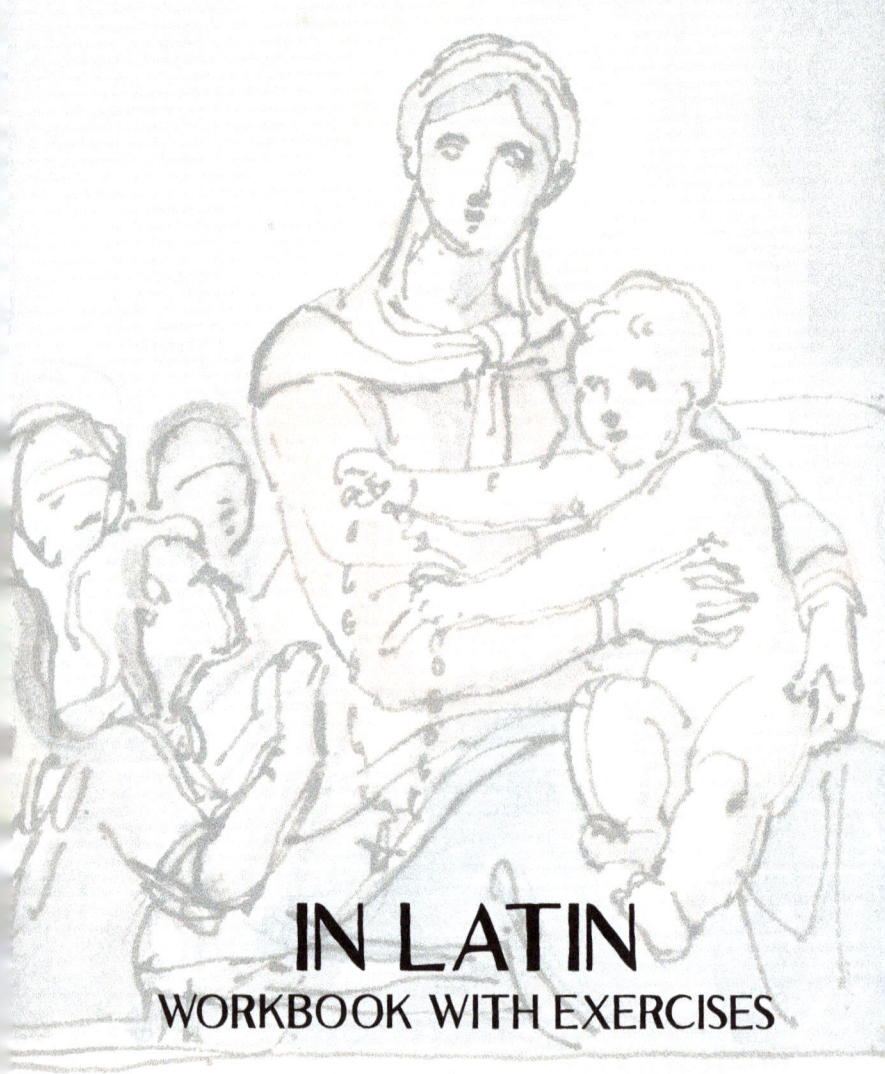

IN LATIN
WORKBOOK WITH EXERCISES

Gloria
Pater Noster
& 2^d Mystery

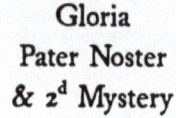

Ave Maria (X10)

Ave Maria (X10)

Gloria
Pater Noster
& 3^d Mystery

Pater Noster
& 1st Mystery

Gloria

5th

4th

Ave Maria (X3)

Pater Noster

Credo

After the 5th Mystery
Salve Regina
(Optional) Oremus

Signum Crucis

Prayers Of The Rosary

SIGNUM CRUCIS

In nomine Patris et Filii et Spiritus Sancti. Amen.

CREDO

Credo in Deum, Patrem omnipotentem, creatorem caeli et terrae. Et in Iesum Christum, Filium eius unicum, Dominum nostrum, qui conceptus est de Spiritu Sancto, natus ex Maria Virgine, passus sub Pontio Pilato, crucifixus, mortuus et sepultus. Descendit ad inferos, tertia die resurrexit a mortuis. Ascendit ad caelos, sedet ad dextram Dei Patris omnipotentis. Inde venturus est iudicare vivos et mortuos. * Credo in Spiritum Sanctum, sanctam Ecclesiam catholicam, sanctorum communionem, remissionem peccatorum, carnis resurrectionem, vitam aeternam. Amen.

PATER NOSTER

Pater noster, qui es in caelis: Sanctificetur nomen tuum: Adveniat regnum tuum: Fiat voluntas tua, sicut in caelo, et in terra. * Panem nostrum quotidianum da nobis hodie: Et dimitte nobis debita nostra, sicut et nos dimittimus debitoribus nostris. Et ne nos inducas in tentationem, sed libera nos a malo. Amen.

AVE MARIA

Ave Maria, gratia plena: Dominus tecum, benedicta tu in mulieribus, et benedictus fructus ventris tui, Iesus. * Sancta Maria, Mater Dei, ora pro nobis peccatoribus, nunc et in hora mortis nostrae. Amen.

GLORIA

Gloria Patri, et Filio, et Spiritui Sancto. * Sicut erat in principio, et nunc, et semper, et in saecula saeculorum. Amen.

ORATIO FATIMAE

Domine Iesu, dimitte nobis debita nostra, salva nos ab igne inferiori, perduc in caelum omnes animas, praesertim eas quae misericordiae tuae maximae indigent.

SALVE REGINA

Salve, Regina, mater misericordiae; vita, dulcedo et spes nostra, salve. Ad te clamamus exsules filii Hevae. Ad te suspiramus gementes et flentes in hac lacrimarum valle. Eia ergo, advocata nostra, illos tuos misericordes oculos ad nos converte. Et Iesum, benedictum fructum ventris tui, nobis post hoc exsilium ostende. O clemens, o pia, o dulcis Virgo Maria.

℣. Ora pro nobis, sancta Dei Genitrix.

℞. Ut digni efficiamur promissionibus Christi.

OREMUS

Deus, cuius Unigenitus per vitam, mortem et resurrectionem suam nobis salutis aeternae praemia comparavit: concede, quaesumus; ut, haec mysteria sacratissimo beatae Mariae Virginis Rosario recolentes. et imitemur quod continent, et quod promittunt, assequamur. Per eundem Christum Dominum nostrum. Amen.

Mysteries Of The Rosary

Mysteria Gaudiosa
Joyful Mysteries

I

Annuntiatiónem Beátæ Maríæ Vírginis
Annunciation of The Blessed Virgin Mary
(Gen. 3:15; Isaias 7:14; St. Luke 1:27; Sirach 24:24-25; St. Luke 1:48; Ps. 44:2)

II

Visitatiónem Beátæ Maríæ Vírginis
Visitation of The Blessed Virgin Mary
(St. Luke 1:43; Josue 3:3-5; St. Luke 1:44, 46, 48; Ps. 44:15, 16)

III

Nativitátem Dómini nostri Iesu Christi
Birth of Our Lord Jesus Christ
(Wisdon 18:14-15; St. John 1:14; St. Luke 7:16; Isaias 9:6)

IV

Oblatiónem Dómini nostri Iesu Christi
Presentation of Our Lord Jesus Christ
(St. Luke 2:30, 32, 34; St. Matthew 10:34; Ps. 116; Ps. 47:10-11)

V

Inventiónem Dómini nostri Iesu Christi in templo
Finding of Our Lord Jesus Christ In The Temple
(St. Luke 2:49, 51 7:16; Ps. 83:2-3)

Mysteria Dolorosa
Sorrowful Mysteries

I

Agóniam Dómini nostri Iesu Christi in horto
Agony of Our Lord Jesus Christ In The Garden
(Hebrews 9:22; Lamentations 1:12; Ps. 21:8-9)

II

Flagellatiónem Dómini nostri Iesu Christi
Scourging of Our Lord Jesus Christ
(Isias 53:5; Apocalypse 5:9-10; Ps. 88:2)

III

Coronatiónem spinis Dómini nostri Iesu Christi
Crowning of Thorns of Our Lord Jesus Christ
(Leviticus 16:20-22; St. John 11:50; 19:15; Daniel 7:13-14; Ps. 8:6-7)

IV

Bajulatiónem Crucis
Carrying of The Cross
(Genesis 3:14, 17-18; 22:6-8; Isias 53:4; 9:6)

V

Crucifixiónem Dómini nostri Iesu Christi
Crucifixion of Our Lord Jesus Christ
(Ps. 21:17; Mark 15:27; John 19:26-27; Lam. 2:13; Matt. 27:54;
Vidi Aquam [cf. Ezekial 47:1])

Mysteria Rosarii

I

Resurrectiónem Dómini nostri Iesu Christi a mórtuis
Resurrection of Our Lord Jesus Christ From The Dead
(Apocalypse 21:5; St. John 2:19; St. Luke 24:35; St. John 20:28; 6:59; Ps. 67:2)

II

Ascensiónem Dómini nostri Iesu Christi in cáelum
Ascension of Our Lord Jesus Christ Into Heaven
(St. Matthew 28:18-20; Ps. 84:11; 44:2)

III

Missiónem Spíritus Sancti in discípulos
Sending of The Holy Spirit To The Disciples
(Joel 2:28-29; Leviticus 16:2; Exodus 25:22; Romans 8:16; Galatians 4:7; Ps. 103:30)

IV

Assumptiónem Beátæ Maríæ Vírginis in cælum
Assumption of The Blessed Virgin Mary Into Heaven
(Apoc. 11:19; St. Luke 1:46; Proverbs 8:22-23, 32-33; St. John 2:5; [Deut. 32:29]; Ps. 44:18)

V

Coronatiónem Beátæ Maríæ Vírginis in cælum
Coronation of The Blessed Virgin Mary In Heaven
(Genesis 3:15; Apocalypse 12:1; Judith 13:18, 23-24, 31; Ps. 44:10;15-16; Ps. 97:1)

I

Baptismum Iordane in flumine
Baptism in the river Jordan
(2 Corinthians 5:21; St. Matthew 3:13)

II

Miraculum Matrimonii Canensis
The miracle of the wedding at Cana
(St. John 2:1-12)

III

Proclamationem Regni Dei
Proclamation of the Kingdom of God
(St. Mark 1:15; 2:3-13; St. Luke 7:47-48; St. John 20:22-23)

IV

Transfigurationem Dómini nostri Iesu Christi
The Transfiguration of Our Lord Jesus Christ
(St. Luke 9:35)

V

Institutionem Eucharistiae
The institution of the Eucharist
(St. John 13:1)

Guide For Praying

ORATIONES AD INCEPTUM

In nomine Patris, et Filio, et Spiritus Sancti
Amen
Credo
Pater Noster
Ave Maria (x3)
Gloria Patri

IN FERIA SECUNDA ET SABBATO

Mysteria Gaudiosa

Contemplamur mysterium gaudiosum:
1: Annuntiatiónis Beátæ Maríæ Vírginis
2: Visitatiónis Beátæ Maríæ Vírginis
3: Nativitátis Dómini nostri Iesu Christi
4: Oblatiónis Dómini nostri Iesu Christi
5: Inventiónis Dómini nostri Iesu Christi in templo

IN FERIA QUINTA

Mysteria Luminosa

Contemplamur mysterium luminosam:
1: Baptismi Iordane in flumine
2: Miraculi Matrimonii Canensis
3: Proclamationis Regni Dei
4: Transfigurationis Dómini nostri Iesu Christi
5: Institutionis Eucharistiae

IN FERIA TERTIA ET FERIA SEXTA

Mysteria Dolorosa

Contemplamur mysterium dolorosam:
1: Agóniae Dómini nostri Iesu Christi in horto
2: Flagellatiónis Dómini nostri Iesu Christi
3: Coronatiónis spinis Dómini nostri Iesu Christi
4: Bajulatiónis Crucis
5: Crucifixiónis Dómini nostri Iesu Christi

IN FERIA QUARTA ET DOMINICA

Mysteria Gloriosa

Contemplamur mysterium gloriosam:
1: Resurrectiónis Dómini nostri Iesu Christi a mórtuis
2: Ascensiónis Dómini nostri Iesu Christi in cáelum
3: Missióni Spíritus Sancti in discípulos
4: Assumptiónis Beátæ Maríæ Vírginis in cælum
5: Coronatiónis Beátæ Maríæ Vírginis in cælum

ORATIONES AD FINEM ROSARII

Salve Regina
Oremus
In nomine Patris, et Filio, et Spiritus Sancti
Amen

The Holy Rosary

PRAYERS AT THE BEGINNING

ON MONDAYS AND SATURDAYS

Joyful Mysteries

We contemplate the joyful mystery of:
1: The Annunciation of The Blessed Virgin Mary
2: The Visitation of The Blessed Virgin Mary
3: The birth of Our Lord Jesus Christ
4: The Presentation of Our Lord Jesus Christ
5: The Finding of Our Lord Jesus Chirst In The Temple

ON THURSDAYS

Luminous Mysteries

We contemplate the luminous mystery of:
1: Christ's Baptism In The River Jordan
2: The Miracle At The Wedding At Cana
3: The Proclomation of The Kingdom of God
4: The Transfiguration of Our Lord Jesus Christ
5: The Institution of The Holy Eucharist

ON TUESDAYS AND FRIDAYS

Sorrowful Mysteries

We contemplate the sorrowful mystery of:
1: The Agony In The Garden of Our Lord Jesus Christ
2: The Scourging of Our Lord Jesus Christ
3: The Coronation of Our Lord Jesus Christ With Thorns
4: Our Lord Jesus Christ Carries The Cross
5: The Crucifixion of Our Lord Jesus Christ

ON WEDNESDAYS AND SUNDAYS

Glorious Mysteries

We contemplate the glorious mystery of:
1: The Resurrection of Our Lord Jesus Christ From The Dead
2: The Ascension of Our Lord Jesus Christ Into Heaven
3: The Descent of The Holy Spirit Into The Disciples
4: The Assumption of The Blessed Virgin Mary Into Heaven
5: The Coronation of The Blessed Virgin Mary In Heaven

PRAYERS AT THE END OF THE ROSARY

THE LATIN LANGUAGE

Roughly speaking there are two common ways to pronounce words in Latin: the Classical way, similar to how Cicero, Julius Caesar, and Virgil spoke, and the Ecclesiastical way, the standard pronunciation of the Church from the late Antique period onward which is the pronunciation that the Church uses to this day. Here we have the Ecclesiastical pronunciation with some brief rules on how Latin vowels and consonants may differ in sound from the ones you may know.

It should be noted that Latin is also a case language, meaning that the ends of nouns change depending on how they are being used. If you are new to Latin this may be unfamiliar but should not be intimidating. A full glossary is included in the back of this book to help with understanding any of the individual words contained in these prayers.

LATIN VOWELS

Letter	Pronunciation	Example
A	AH	(AH)d-vo-kah-tah *Advocata*
E	EH	(EH)-ksoo-les *Exsules*
I	EE	(EE)n-deh *Inde*
O	OH	(OH) *O*
U	OO	(OO)t *Ut*
Y	I	M(I)-steh-ree-ah *Mysteria*
AE	AY	(AY)-ter-nam *Aeternam*
Q+UA/E/I/O	KWA/EH/EE/OH	(KWEE)-s-(KWEH) *Quisque*
AU	OW	(OW)t *Aut*

SPECIAL LATIN CONSONANTS

Letter	Pronunciation	Example
C + Consonants	K	(K)lah-mah-moos *Clamamus*
C + E, AE, OE, I	CH	(CH)ay-lum *Caelum*
C + A, O, U	K	(K)ar-nis *Carnis*
G + A, O, U	G	(G)aw-deh-teh *Gaudete*
G + E, I	J	(J)eh-neh-trix *Genetrix*
H	Silent (except for between vowels)	Nee-(H)il *Nihil*
J/I	Y	(Y)eh-soos *Jesus*
CH	K	(K)ri-stoos *Christus*
GN	NY	Di-(NY)oom *Dignum*
PH	F	Pro-(F)eh-tes *Prophetes*
TH	T	Ka-(T)o-li-kam *Catholicam*
SC + E, I	SH	(SH)ee-ents-ee-ah *Scientia*
CC + E, I	TCH	Eh-(TCH)eh *Ecce*
TI + Any Vowel	TSI	Grah-(TSI)-ah *Gratia*
XC + E, I	KSH	Eh-(KSH)el-sis *Excelsis*
Z	DZ	Bap-tee-(DZ)o *Baptizo*

SIGNUM CRUCIS

THE SIGN OF THE CROSS

In nomine Patris

In the name of the Father,

et Filii et Spiritus Sancti.

and of the Son, and of the Holy Spirit.

Amen.

Amen.

In nomine _____

et _____ et Spiritus _____.

Amen.

1. **Patris**

2. **Filii   Sancti**

3.

__ nomine _____

et _____ et _____ _____.

Amen.

1.   In   Patris

2. Filii   Spiritus   Sancti

3.

___ _____ _____

et _____ **et** _____ _____.

_____.

1.   In nomine   Patris

2. Filii   Spiritus   Sancti

3.   Amen

_____ _____ _____

___ _____ _____ ___ _____ _____ _____ •

_____ •

1. Patris In nomine

2. et Spiritus Filii et Sancti

3. Amen

In the name of the Father,

and of the Son, and of the Holy Spirit.

Amen.

All Words

Filii et Spiritus nomine

In   Amen   Patris

et Sancti

In nomine Patris

et Filii et Spiritus Sancti.

Amen.

REFLECTION

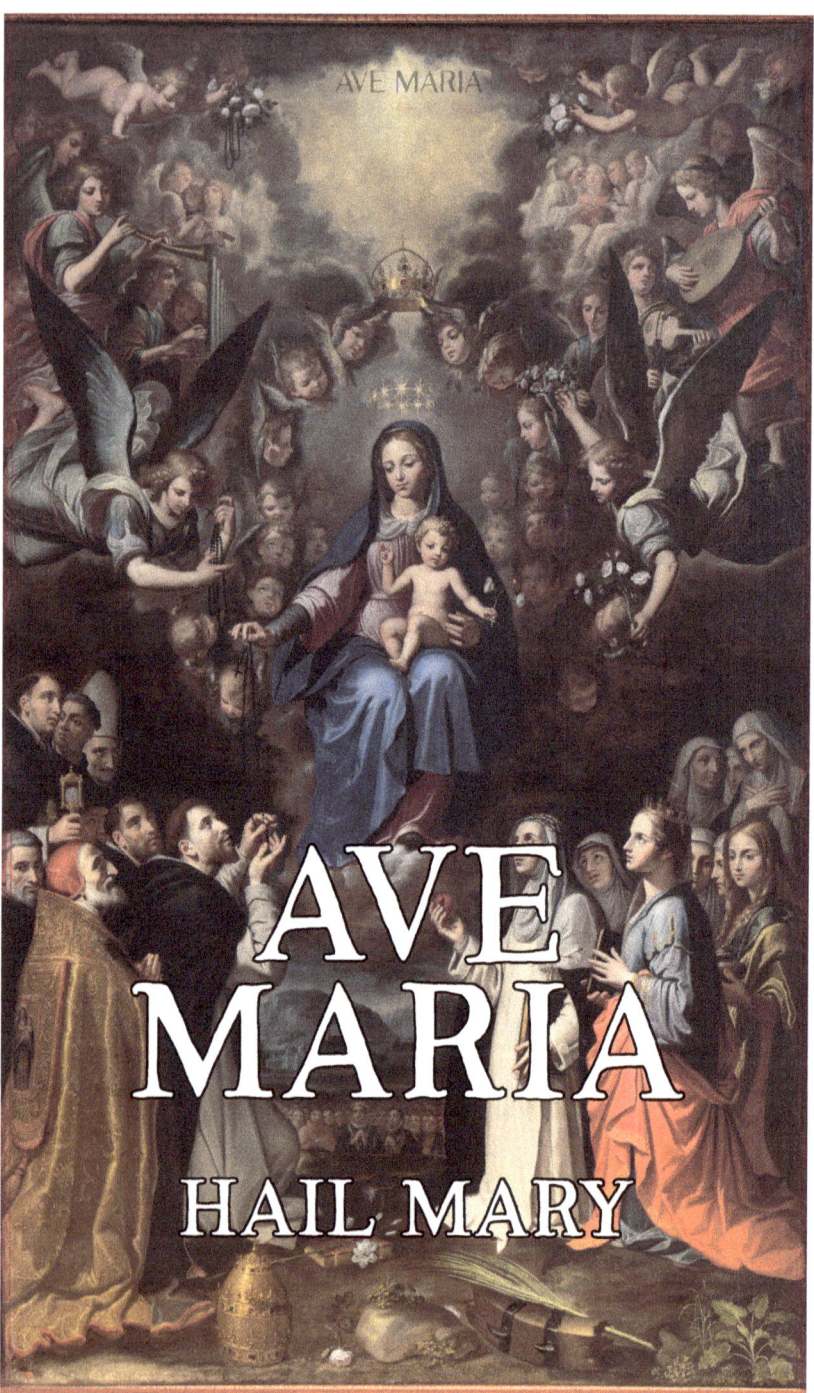

AVE MARIA

AVE
MARIA
HAIL MARY

Ave Maria, gratia plena,
Hail, Mary, full of grace,

Dominus tecum.
the Lord is with thee.

Benedicta tu in mulieribus
blessed art thou among women

et benedictus fructus
and blessed is the fruit

ventris tui,
of thy womb,

Iesus.
Jesus.

Sancta Maria,
Holy Mary,

Mater Dei,
Mother of God,

ora pro nobis
pray for us

peccatoribus
sinners

nunc et in hora
now and at the hour

mortis nostrae.
of our death.

Amen.
Amen.

Ave Maria, _____ plena,

Dominus _____.

_____ tu in mulieribus

et benedictus _____

ventris tui,

_____.

Sancta _____,

_____ Dei,

ora ___ nobis

_____

_____ et in hora

mortis _____.

Amen.

1   gratia

2   tecum

3   benedicta

4   fructus

5

6   Iesus

7   Maria

8   Mater

9   pro

10   peccatoribus

11   nunc

12   nostrae

13

___ Maria, _____ plena,

Dominus _____.

_____ tu in _____

__ benedictus _____

_____ tui,

_____.

_____ ____,

_____ Dei,

ora ___ _____

_____

____ et in ____

_____ _____.

Amen.

1 Ave   gratia

2   tecum

3   benedicta   mulieribus

4   et   fructus

5   ventris

6   Iesus

7   Sancta   Maria

8   Mater

9   pro   nobis

10   peccatoribus

11   nunc   hora

12   mortis   nostrae

13

AVE MARIA

1 Ave Maria gratia plena

2 Dominus tecum

3 benedicta tu in mulieribus

4 et benedictus fructus

5 ventris tui

6 Iesus

7 Sancta Maria

8 Mater Dei

9 ora pro nobis

10 peccatoribus

11 nunc et in hora

12 mortis nostrae

13 Amen

——— ————, ———— ————,

———— ———•

—————— —— —— ——————

—— ————— ——— ————

————— ———,

————•

————— ————,

———— ———,

——— ——— ———

——————

———— ——— ——— ————

————— —————•

————•

1 Maria Ave plena gratia

2 tecum Dominus

3 tu in benedicta mulieribus

4 fructus benedictus et

5 tui ventris

6 Iesus

7 Maria   Sancta

8 Dei   Mater

9 pro   ora   nobis

10   peccatoribus

11 et nunc hora in

12 nostrae   mortis

13 Amen

AVE MARIA

———— ———— , ———— ————,
Hail, Mary, full of grace,

———— ————.
the Lord is with thee.

———— ——— —— ————
blessed art thou among women

—— ———— ——— ————
and blessed is the fruit

———— ——,
of thy womb,

————.
Jesus.

———— ————,
Holy Mary,

———— ————,
Mother of God,

——— ——— ————
pray for us

————————
sinners

——— ——— —— ————
now and at the hour

———— ————.
of our death.

————.
Amen.

42

All Words

Ave   Iesus.   nobis

Maria   tecum   plena:

benedicta   Sancta   tu

tui   Maria   benedictus

gratia   Dominus   hora

nunc   mortis   in

in   fructus   et

Dei   peccatoribus   pro

Mater   nostrae.   ora

Amen.   mulieribus   et

ventris

Ave Maria, gratia plena,

Dominus tecum.

Benedicta tu in mulieribus

et benedictus fructus

ventris tui,

Iesus.

Sancta Maria,

Mater Dei,

ora pro nobis

peccatoribus

nunc et in hora

mortis nostrae.

Amen.

REFLECTION

PATER
NOSTER

OUR FATHER

Pater noster,
Our Father,

qui es in caelis,
Who art in heaven,

sanctificetur nomen tuum.
hallowed be Thy name.

Adveniat regnum tuum.
Thy kingdom come.

Fiat voluntas tua,
Thy will be done,

sicut in caelo, et in terra.
just as it is in heaven, so also on Earth.

Panem nostrum quotidianum
Our daily bread

da nobis hodie
give to us this day

et dimitte nobis
and forgive us

debita nostra,
our debts,

sicut et nos dimittimus
just as we forgive

debitoribus nostris.
our debtors.

Et ne nos inducas in tentationem,
And lead us not into temptation;

sed libera nos a malo.
but deliver us from evil.

Amen.
Amen.

_____ noster,

qui __ in _____,

sanctificetur _____ tuum.

_____ regnum tuum.

Fiat voluntas ___,

_____ in caelo, __ in terra.

Panem nostrum _____

__ nobis hodie

et _____ nobis

_____ nostra,

sicut __ nos _____

_____ nostris.

__ ne nos inducas in

_____,

sed _____ nos a ___.

Amen.

LEVEL 1 - FEW WORDS MISSING

1   Pater

2   es   caelis

3   nomen

4   Adveniat

5   tua

6   sicut   et

7   quotidianum

8   da

9   dimitte

10 debita

11 et   dimittimus

12 debitoribus

13 Et

14 tentationem

15 libera   malo

16

_____ noster,

___ __ in _____,

_____ _____ tuum.

_____ regnum ____.

____ voluntas ___,

_____ in _____, __ in _____.

_____ nostrum _____

__ nobis _____

__ _____ nobis

_____ _____,

_____ __ nos _____

_____ nostris.

__ ne nos _____ in

_____,

sed _____ ___ a ____.

Amen.

1 Pater

2 qui   es   caelis

3 Sanctificetur   nomen

4 Adveniat   tuum

5 Fiat   tua

6 sicut   caelo   et   terra

7 Panem   quotidianum

8 da   hodie

9 Et   dimitte

10 debita   nostra

11 sicut   et   dimittimus

12 debitoribus

13 Et   inducas

14 tentationem

15 libera   nos   malo

16

1   Pater   noster

2   qui   es   in   caelis

3   Sanctificetur nomen tuum

4   Adveniat   regnum tuum

5   Fiat   voluntas   tua

6   sicut   in caelo et in terra

7 Panem nostrum quotidianum

8   da   nobis   hodie

9   Et   dimitte nobis

10   debita   nostra

11   sicut   et   nos dimittimus

12   debitoribus   nostris

13   Et   ne   nos inducas in

14   tentationem

15   sed libera   nos a malo

16   Amen

PATER NOSTER

—— ——,

—— —— —— ——,

———————— —— ——.

—————— ———— ——.

—— ———— ——,

———— —— ——, —— —— ——.

—— ———— ————

—— —— —— ——

—— —— —— ——

———— ——,

—— —— —— ————

———————— ————.

—— —— —— ———— ——.

———————— ,

—— ———— —— — ——.

——.

LEVEL 4 - EACH LINE JUMBLED

1. noster Pater
2. es qui caelis in
3. nomen Sanctificetur tuum
4. tuum Adveniat regnum
5. voluntas tua Fiat
6. caelo sicut terra in et in
7. Panem quotidianum nostrum
8. nobis da hodie
9. nobis Et dimitte
10. nostra debita
11. sicut dimittimus et nos
12. nostris debitoribus
13. inducas Et ne nos in
14. tentationem
15. libera sed malo a nos
16. Amen

PATER NOSTER

_____ _____,
Our Father,

_____ ____ __ _____,
Who art in heaven,

_____ ___ _____ ____.
hallowed be Thy name.

_____ _____ _____.
Thy kingdom come.

____ _____ ____,
Thy will be done,

_____ __ _____, __ __ _____.
just as it is in heaven, so also on Earth.

_____ _____ _____
Our daily bread

__ _____ _____
give to us this day

__ _____ _____
and forgive us

_____ _____,
our debts,

_____ __ _____
just as we forgive

_____ _____.
our debtors.

__ __ ____ _____ __ _____,
And lead us not into temptation;

___ _____ ____ __ ____.
but deliver us from evil.

____.
Amen.

All Words

tua   sicut   Fiat   debita

nobis hodie: quotidianum

debitoribus qui   es   Pater

nomen   nostra   sicut   nobis

in nostris.   Et   nos   in

tuum: Adveniat   Sanctificetur

terra.   et   da

tentationem   sed inducas noster

Amen.   a   malo.   caelo

in   in   caelis: nos

Panem   regnum tuum: dimitte

Et   ne   et   nos

libera   nostrum

voluntas   dimittimus

Pater noster,

qui es in caelis,

sanctificetur nomen tuum.

Adveniat regnum tuum.

Fiat voluntas tua,

sicut in caelo, et in terra.

Panem nostrum quotidianum

da nobis hodie

et dimitte nobis

debita nostra,

sicut et nos dimittimus

debitoribus nostris.

Et ne nos inducas in tentationem,

sed libera nos a malo.

Amen.

REFLECTION

CREDO

I BELIEVE

FULL PRAYER

Credo in Deum, Patrem omnipotentem,
I believe in God the Father Almighty,

creatorem caeli et terrae.
Creator of heaven and earth.

Et in Iesum Christum, Filium eius unicum,
And in Jesus Christ, His only Son,

Dominum nostrum, qui conceptus est de Spiritu Sancto,
our Lord, Who was conceived by the Holy Spirit,

natus ex Maria Virgine, passus sub Pontio Pilato,
born of the Virgin Mary, suffered under Pontius Pilate,

crucifixus, mortuus et sepultus.
was crucified, died and was buried.

Descendit ad inferos, tertia die resurrexit a mortuis.
He descended into hell, the third day He rose from the dead.

Ascendit ad caelos,
He ascended into heaven

sedet ad dextram Dei Patris omnipotentis.
and sits at the right hand of God, the Father Almighty.

Inde venturus est iudicare vivos et mortuos.
From thence He shall come to judge the living and the dead.

Credo in Spiritum Sanctum,
I believe the Holy Spirit,

sanctam Ecclesiam catholicam,
the holy Catholic Church,

sanctorum communionem,
the communion of saints,

remissionem peccatorum, carnis resurrectionem,
the forgiveness of sins, the resurrection of the body,

vitam aeternam.
and life everlasting.

Amen.

Credo in _____, Patrem _____,

_____ caeli et terrae.

Et in _____ Christum, _____ eius unicum,

_____ nostrum, qui conceptus est de _____ Sancto,

natus ex _____ Virgine, _____ sub Pontio Pilato,

_____, mortuus et sepultus.

Descendit ad _____, tertia die _____ a mortuis.

_____ ad caelos,

sedet ad _____ Dei _____ omnipotentis.

Inde _____ est _____ vivos et mortuos.

_____ in Spiritum _____,

sanctam _____ catholicam,

sanctorum _____,

_____ peccatorum, carnis _____,

_____ aeternam.

Amen.

LEVEL I - FEW WORDS MISSING

1 Deum   omnipotentem

2   creatorem

3 Iesum   Filium

4 Dominum   Spiritu

5   Maria   passus

6 crucifixus

7   inferos   resurrexit

8 Ascendit

9 dextram   Patris

10   venturus   iudicare

11 Credo   Sanctum

12   Ecclesiam

13   communionem

14 remissionem   resurrectionem

15 vitam

16

Credo in ____, _____ _____,

_____ _____ et _____.

Et in _____ _____, _____ eius _____,

_____ nostrum, qui _____ est de _____ _____,

_____ ex _____ _____, _____ sub Pontio _____,

_____, _____ et _____.

_____ ad _____, tertia die _____ a mortuis.

_____ ad _____,

_____ ad _____ Dei _____ _____.

Inde _____ est _____ _____ et _____.

_____ in _____ _____,

_____ _____ _____,

sanctorum _____,

_____ _____, carnis _____,

_____ _____.

____.

LEVEL 2 - MORE WORDS MISSING

1   Deum   Patrem   omnipotentem

2   creatorem   caeli   terrae

3   Iesum Christum   Filium   unicum

4   Dominum   conceptus   Spiritu   Sancto

5   natus   Maria   Virgine   passus   Pilato

6   crucifixus   mortuus   sepultus

7   Descendit   inferos   resurrexit

8   Ascendit   caelos

9   sedet   dextram   Patris   omnipotentis

10   venturus   iudicare   vivos   mortuos

11   Credo   Sanctum   Spiritum

12   sanctam   Ecclesiam   catholicam

13   communionem

14   remissionem   peccatorum   resurrectionem

15   vitam   aeternam

16   Amen

CREDO

———— —— ————, ———— ——————,

———————— ———— —— ————.

—— —— ———— ————, ———— —— ————,

———— ————, —— ———————— —— ———— ————,

———— —— ———— ————, ———— —— ———— ————,

———————— ————, ———— —— ————.

———— —— ————, ———— —— ———— —— ————.

———————— —— ————,

———— —— ———— ———— ——————.

—— ———————— ———— ———— —— ————.

———— —— ———— ————,

———— ———— ———— ————,

———— ——————,

———————— ————————, ———— ——————,

———— ————.

———.

LEVEL 3 - WRITE EACH LINE

1 Credo in Deum   Patrem   omnipotentem

2   creatorem   caeli   et terrae

3 Et in Iesum Christum   Filium eius   unicum

4 Dominum nostrum qui conceptus est de Spiritu Sancto

5 natus ex Maria   Virgine passus sub Pontio Pilato

6 crucifixus   mortuus et   sepultus

7 Descendit ad inferos tertia die resurrexit a mortuis

8 Ascendit   ad   caelos

9 sedet ad dextram   Dei Patris omnipotentis

10 Inde venturus est iudicare   vivos   et   mortuos

11 Credo in   Sanctum   Spiritum

12 sanctam   Ecclesiam   catholicam

13   sanctorum communionem

14 remissionem peccatorum carnis resurrectionem

15 vitam aeternam

16 Amen

CREDO

———— —— ————, ———— ——————————,

———————— ———— —— ————.

—— —— ———— —————, ———— ———— ————,

—————— ————, —— ——————— —— ———— ————,

————— —— ————, ———— ——— ———— ————,

——————, ———— —— ————.

————— —— ————, ————— ——————— —— ————.

——————————,

————— —— —————————— —————.

——— ——————————— —— ————.

———— —— ———— ————,

————— ——————— —————,

————— —————,

————— —————, ———— —————,

———— ————.

————.

LEVEL 4 - EACH LINE JUMBLED

1 in Deum Credo   omnipotentem Patrem

2   caeli   creatorem terrae et

3 Christum Et in   Filium Iesum eius   unicum

4 Dominum Spiritu qui conceptus nostrum est de Sancto

5 Maria natus   ex   passus Virgine Pilato Pontio sub

6 sepultus et crucifixus   mortuus

7 a inferos Descendit resurrexit ad mortuis   tertia die

8 ad caelos Ascendit

9 dextram sedet ad omnipotentis Dei Patris

10 venturus Inde est   vivos   iudicare et   mortuos

11 Sanctum Credo   in   Spiritum

12 catholicam   sanctam   Ecclesiam

13   communionem sanctorum

14 carnis resurrectionem remissionem peccatorum

15 aeternam vitam

16 Amen

CREDO

——— —— ———, ——— ————————,
I believe in God the Father Almighty,

———— ——— —— ———.
Creator of heaven and earth.

—— —— ——— ———, ——— —— ———,
And in Jesus Christ, His only Son,

——— ———, — ———— —— ——— ———,
our Lord, Who was conceived by the Holy Spirit,

——— —— ——— ———, ——— —— ———,
born of the Virgin Mary, suffered under Pontius Pilate,

———, ——— —— ———.
was crucified, died and was buried.

——— —— ———, ——— ——— ——— — ———.
He descended into hell, the third day He rose from the dead.

——— —— ———,
He ascended into heaven

——— —— ——— — ——— ———.
and sits at the right hand of God, the Father Almighty.

——— ——— ——— ——— —— ———.
From thence He shall come to judge the living and the dead.

——— —— ——— ———,
I believe the Holy Spirit,

——— ——— ———,
the holy Catholic Church,

——— ———,
the communion of saints,

——— ———, ———. ——— ———,
the forgiveness of sins, the resurrection of the body,

——— ———.
and life everlasting.

———.

All Words

Virgine,   peccatorum,   terrae.

Et caelos,   sedet   venturus   Pontio

est   Sancto,   natus vivos conceptus

Sanctum   in Deum, iudicare Christum

sanctam carnis mortuus Ecclesiam qui et Pilato

sub   crucifixus, a   omnipotentem,

creatorem   tertia Iesum inferos, et Spiritu ad

communionem,   remissionem   unicum,

die   aeternam.   Dominum nostrum, Dei passus

Amen.   Patrem sepultus.   resurrectionem,

Descendit   de resurrexit   Patris mortuos.

Credo   Maria Spiritum   vitam

Inde in ad dextram in mortuis.   catholicam,

Ascendit et caeli ad est Credo Filium eius ex

sanctorum   omnipotentis.

CREDO

Credo in Deum, Patrem omnipotentem,

creatorem caeli et terrae.

Et in Iesum Christum, Filium eius unicum,

Dominum nostrum, qui conceptus est de Spiritu Sancto,

natus ex Maria Virgine, passus sub Pontio Pilato,

crucifixus, mortuus et sepultus.

Descendit ad inferos, tertia die resurrexit a mortuis.

Ascendit ad caelos,

sedet ad dextram Dei Patris omnipotentis.

Inde venturus est iudicare vivos et mortuos.

Credo in Spiritum Sanctum,

sanctam Ecclesiam catholicam,

sanctorum communionem,

remissionem peccatorum, carnis resurrectionem,

vitam aeternam.

Amen.

REFLECTION

GLORIA
PATRI

GLORY BE

Gloria Patri,
Glory be to the Father,

et Filio,
and to the Son,

et Spiritui Sancto.
and to the Holy Spirit.

Sicut erat in principio,
As it was in the beginning,

et nunc, et semper,
is now, and is always,

et in saecula saeculorum.
and is unto ages of ages.

Amen.
Amen.

_____ Patri,

et _____,

et Spiritui _____.

_____ erat in principio,

et ____, et semper,

et in saecula _____.

Amen.

1.   Gloria

2.   Filio

3.   Sancto

4.   Sicut

5.   nunc

6.   saeculorum

7.

_____ _____,

et _____,

et _____ _____.

_____ erat in _____,

et ____, et _____,

et in _____ _____.

_____.

1. Gloria   Patri

2. Filio

3. Spiritui   Sancto

4. Sicut   principio

5. nunc   semper

6. saecula   saeculorum

7. Amen

————— —————,

—— —————,

—— ————— —————•

————— —— —— —————,

—— —————, —— —————,

—— —— ————— —————•

—————•

1. Gloria   Patri

2. et Filio

3. et Spiritui   Sancto

4. Sicut erat in principio

5. et nunc   et semper

6. et in saecula saeculorum

7. Amen

1.   Patri Gloria

2.   Filio et

3.   Spiritui et   Sancto

4. erat principio in Sicut

5.   semper et nunc et

6. in saeculorum et saecula

7.   Amen

———— ————,
Glory be to the Father,

—— ————,
and to the Son,

—— ———————— ————.
and to the Holy Spirit.

———————— ———— —— ————,
As it was in the beginning,

—— ————, —— ————,
is now, and is always,

—— —— ———— ————————.
and is unto ages of ages.

————.
Amen.

All Words

saeculorum semper et et

Patri et principio et

Gloria saecula Sancto

Sicut in in nunc Spiritui

Amen   erat Filio   et

Gloria Patri,

et Filio,

et Spiritui Sancto.

Sicut erat in principio,

et nunc, et semper,

et in saecula saeculorum.

Amen.

REFLECTION

SALVE REGINA

HAIL, HOLY QUEEN

Salve, Regina,
Hail, holy Queen,

mater misericordiae;
Mother of mercy,

vita, dulcedo et spes nostra,
our life, our sweetness and our hope.

salve.
Hail.

Ad te clamamus exsules filii Hevae.
To thee do we cry, poor banished children of Eve.

Ad te suspiramus gementes et flentes
To thee do we sigh, mourning and weeping

in hac lacrimarum valle.
in this valley of tears.

Eia ergo, advocata nostra,
Therefore, our advocate,

illos tuos misericordes oculos
thine eyes of mercy

ad nos converte.
turn toward us.

Et Iesum,
And Jesus,

benedictum fructum ventris tui,
the blessed fruit of thy womb,

nobis post hoc exsilium ostende.
after this, our exile, show unto us.

O clemens, o pia, o dulcis
O clement, O loving, O sweet

Virgo Maria.
Virgin Mary.

℣. Ora pro nobis,
℣. Pray for us,

sancta Dei Genitrix.
O holy Mother of God.

℞. Ut digni efficiamur
℞. That we may be made worthy

promissionibus Christi.
of the promises of Christ.

Salve, _____,

_____ misericordiae;

vita, _____ et spes _____,

salve.

Ad te _____ exsules filii _____.

Ad te suspiramus _____ et _____in hac

_____ valle.

___ ergo, _____ nostra,

illos tuos _____ _____

ad nos _____.

Et _____,

_____ fructum _____ tui,

_____ post hoc exsilium _____.

O _____, o ___, o dulcis

_____ Maria.

℣. ___ pro nobis,

_____ Dei _____.

℟. Ut _____ efficiamur

_____ Christi.

1   Regina

2   mater

3   dulcedo   nostra

4

5   clamamus Hevae

6   gementes flentes

7   lacrimarum

8   Eia   advocata

9   misericordes   oculos

10   converte

11 Iesum

12   benedictum   ventris

13   nobis   ostende

14   clemens   pia

15 Virgo

16   Ora

17 sancta   Genitrix

18 digni

19 promissionibus

_____, _____,

_____ _____;

____, _____ et ____ _____,

salve.

Ad te _____ exsules _____ ____.

Ad te _____ _____ et _____in

hac _____ ____.

___ ergo, _____ _____,

_____ tuos _____ _____

ad ___ _____.

Et _____,

_____ _____ _____ tui,

_____ post hoc _____ _____.

O _____, o ___, o _____

_____ ____.

℣. ___ ___ nobis,

_____ __ _____.

℞. Ut _____ _____

_____ _____.

1   Salve   Regina

2   mater   misericordiae

3   vita   dulcedo   spes   nostra

4

5   clamamus   filii   Hevae

6   suspiramus   gementes   flentes

7   lacrimarum   valle

8   Eia   advocata   nostra

9   illos   misericordes   oculos

10   nos   converte

11   Iesum

12   benedictum   fructum   ventris

13   nobis   exsilium   ostende

14   clemens   pia   dulcis

15   Virgo   Maria

16   Ora   pro

17   sancta   Dei   Genitrix

18   digni   efficiamur

19   promissionibus   Christi

——— , ——— ,

——— ——————— ;

——— , ——— — — — ——— ,

——— .

— — — ——— ——— ——— .

— — ——————— — — ——— —

——— ——— ——— .

— ——— , ——— — ——— ,

——— — — ——————— ———

— — ——— .

— ——— ,

——————— ——— ——— ——— ,

——— — — — ——— ——— .

— ——— , — — ——— , — — ———

——— ——— .

℣. — ——— — ——— ,

——— — — ——— .

℞. — — — ——— ———

——————— ——— .

LEVEL 3 - WRITE EACH LINE

1. Salve Regina
2. mater misericordiae
3. vita dulcedo et spes nostra
4. salve
5. ad te clamamus exsules filii Hevae
6. Ad te suspiramus gementes et flentes in
7. hac lacrimarum valle
8. Eia ergo advocata nostra
9. illos tuos misericordes oculos
10. ad nos converte
11. Et Iesum
12. benedictum fructum ventris tui
13. nobis post hoc exsilium ostende
14. O clemens o pia o dulcis
15. Virgo Maria
16. Ora pro nobis
17. sancta Dei Genitrix
18. Ut digni efficiamur
19. promissionibus Christi

SALVE REGINA

_____, _____,
_____ _____;
____, _____ __ ___ _____,
_____.
__ __ _____ _____ _____ _____.
__ __ _____ _____ _____ _____ __
___ _____ _____.
___ ___, _____ _____,
_____ ___ _____ _____
__ ___ _____.
__ _____,
_____ _____ _____ ___,
_____ ___ ___ _____ _____.
_ _____, _ ___, _ _____
_____ ___.

℣. ___ ___ _____,
_____ ___ _____.

℟. __ _____ _____
_____ _____.

LEVEL 4 - EACH LINE JUMBLED

1 Regina Salve

2 misericordiae mater

3 dulcedo vita nostra et spes

4 salve

5 clamamus ad te Hevae exsules filii

6 suspiramus Ad te flentes gementes et in

7 valle hac lacrimarum

8 Eia advocata nostra ergo

9 misericordes illos oculos tuos

10 ad converte nos

11 Iesum Et

12 fructum benedictum tui ventris

13 ostende nobis exsilium post hoc

14 dulcis pia clemens O o o

15 Maria Virgo

16 nobis Ora pro

17 Dei Genitrix sancta

18 digni efficiamur Ut

19 Christi promissionibus

SALVE REGINA

———, ———,
Hail, holy Queen,

——— — ———;
Mother of mercy,

———, ——— —— ——— ———,
our life, our sweetness and our hope.

———•
Hail.

— —— ——— ——— —— ——— ———•
To thee do we cry, poor banished children of Eve.

— — ——— ——— —— ——— — ——— —
To thee do we sigh, mourning and weeping

—— ——— ———•
in this valley of tears.

—— ———, ——— ———,
Therefore, our advocate,

——— ——— ——— ———
thine eyes of mercy

— —— ———•
turn toward us.

— ———,
And Jesus,

——— ——— ——,
the blessed fruit of thy womb,

——— — —— ——— ———•
after this, our exile, show unto us.

— ———, — ———, — ———
O clement, O loving, O sweet

—— ———•
Virgin Mary.

℣. —— —— ———,
V. Pray for us,

——— —— ———•
O holy Mother of God.

℟. —— ——— ———
R. That we may be made worthy

——— ———•
of the promises of Christ.

All Words

valle   Eia   hoc   nobis

sancta   ergo nos   post exsules

hac   te   clemens   lacrimarum

dulcedo   Maria   et   Ora dulcis

Virgo   ventris

Hevae   Ad

exsilium   o   tui   nobis   Iesum

benedictum   Regina   mater

Ut   suspiramus Dei digni

Salve   misericordes te filii   flentes

in   gementes misericordiae;   vita

nostra   salve

Ad fructum nostra

illos o efficiamur

promissionibus advocata

clamamus   oculos   ad pia ostende

O converte

Et Genitrix   pro et tuos spes Christi

Salve, Regina,
mater misericordiae;
vita, dulcedo et spes nostra,
salve.
Ad te clamamus exsules filii Hevae.
Ad te suspiramus gementes et flentes
in hac lacrimarum valle.
Eia ergo, advocata nostra,
illos tuos misericordes oculos
ad nos converte.
Et Iesum,
benedictum fructum ventris tui,
nobis post hoc exsilium ostende.
O clemens, o pia, o dulcis
Virgo Maria.
V. Ora pro nobis,
sancta Dei Genitrix.
R. Ut digni efficiamur
promissionibus Christi.

REFLECTION

ORATIO FATIMAE

FATIMA PRAYER

Domine Iesu,

Lord Jesus,

dimitte nobis debita nostra,

forgive us our sins,

salva nos ab igne inferiori,

save us from the fires of hell,

perduc in caelum omnes animas,

lead all souls to heaven,

praesertim eas quae

especially those who,

misericordiae tuae

of thy mercy,

maximae indigent.

are most in need.

_____ Iesu,

_____ nobis _____ nostra,

salva nos ab igne _____,

_____ in _____ omnes animas,

_____ eas quae

_____ tuae

maximae _____.

1   Domine

2   dimitte   debita

3   inferiori

4   perduc   caelum

5   praesertim

6   misericordiae

7   indigent

_____ ____,

_____ nobis _____ _____,

_____ nos ab ____ _____,

_____ in _____ omnes _____,

_____ eas ____

_____ tuae

_____ _____.

1   Domine   Iesu

2   dimitte   debita   nostra

3   salva   igne   inferiori

4   perduc   caelum   animas

5   praesertim   quae

6   misericordiae

7   maximae   indigent

_____ ____,

_____ ____ ____ ____,

_____ __ __ ____,

_____ __ ____ ____ ____,

_____ ___ ___

_____ ____

_____ _____.

1   Domine   Iesu

2   dimitte nobis debita nostra

3   salva nos ab igne inferiori

4 perduc in caelum omnes animas

5   praesertim   eas quae

6   misericordiae tuae

7   maximae   indigent

ORATIO FATIMAE

_____ ____,

_____ ____ ____ ____,

_____ __ __ ____ _____,

____ __ _____ ____ _____,

_____ ___ ___

_____ ____

_____ _____.

1   Iesu Domine

2   debita nostra dimitte nobis

3   igne ab salva nos inferiori

4 caelum in omnes animas perduc

5   quae praesertim eas

6   tuae misericordiae

7   indigent maximae

_____ _____,

Lord Jesus,

_____ _____ _____ _____,

forgive us our sins,

_____ ____ __ _____ _____,

save us from the fires of hell,

_____ __ _____ _____ _____,

and lead all souls to heaven,

_____ ____ _____

especially those who,

_____ _____

of thy mercy,

_____ _____.

are most in need.

All Words

caelum indigent ab Iesu

dimitte omnes nos nobis in inferiori

perduc eas Domine nostra

salva tuae

maximae animas

praesertim igne debita quae

misericordiae

Domine Iesu,

dimitte nobis debita nostra,

salva nos ab igne inferiori,

perduc in caelum omnes animas,

praesertim eas quae

misericordiae tuae

maximae indigent.

REFLECTION

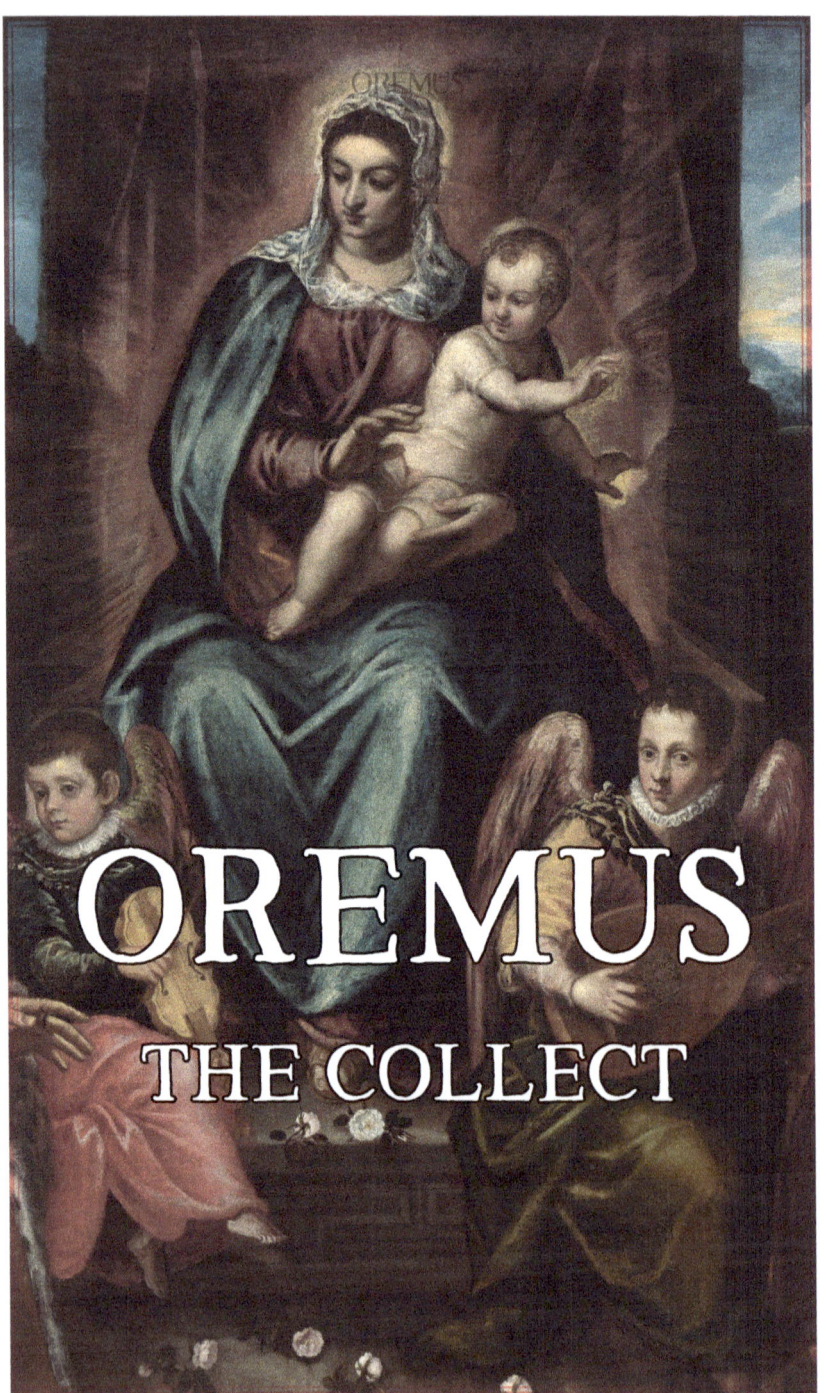

OREMUS

THE COLLECT

Deus,
O God,

cuius Unigenitus per vitam,
Whose Only-Begotten Son, by His life,

mortem et resurrectionem
death and resurrection,

suam nobis salutis aeternae
has for us the rewards of eternal salvation

praemia comparavit:
purchased:

concede, quaesumus;
grant, we beseech Thee,

ut, haec mysteria sacratissimo
that by these mysteries of the most holy Rosary

beatae Mariae Virginis
of the Blessed Virgin Mary,

Rosario recolentes,
meditating on them,

et imitemur quod continent,
we may both imitate what they contain,

et quod promittunt,
and what they promise,

assequamur.
we may obtain.

Per eundem
Through the same

Christum Dominum nostrum.
Christ our Lord.

Amen.
Amen.

_____,

cuius _____ per vitam,

_____ et resurrectionem

____ nobis salutis _____

_____ comparavit:

concede, _____;

ut, ____ mysteria _____

_____ Mariae Virginis

Rosario _____.

et _____ quod _____,

et ____ promittunt,

_____.

___ eundem

_____ Dominum _____.

Amen.

1   Deus
2   Unigenitus
3   mortem
4   suam   aeternae
5   praemia
6   quaesumus
7   haec   sacratissimo
8   beatae
9   recolentes
10 imitemur   continent
11 quod
12   assequamur
13 Per
14 Christum   nostrum
15

____,

cuius _____ per ____,

_____ et _____

___ nobis _____ _____

_____ _____:

concede, _____;

ut, ___ _____ _____

_____ Mariae _____

_____ _____.

et _____ quod _____,

et ___ _____,

_____.

___ ____

_____ Dominum ____.

___.

1 Deus

2 Unigenitus   vitam

3 mortem   resurrectionem

4 suam   salutis   aeternae

5   praemia   comparavit

6 quaesumus

7 haec mysteria sacratissimo

8 beatae   Virginis

9 Rosario   recolentes

10 imitemur   continent

11 quod   promittunt

12   assequamur

13 Per   eundem

14 Christum   nostrum

15 Amen

OREMUS

——,

———— ———————— ——— ————,

————— —— ————————————

——————— ————— ————————— ——————

———————— ————————:

————————, ————————;

——, ————— ———————— ————————————

————— ———————— —————————

————— —————————

—— ———————— ——— ———————,

—— ————— ————————,

———————•

———— ———————

——————— ———————— ——————•

————•

1 Deus

2 cuius Unigenitus per vitam

3 mortem et resurrectionem

4 suam nobis salutis aeternae

5 praemia comparavit

6 concede quaesumus

7 ut haec mysteria sacratissimo

8 beatae Mariae Virginis

9 Rosario recolentes

10 et imitemur quod continent

11 et quod promittunt

12 assequamur

13 Per eundem

14 Christum Dominum nostrum

15 Amen

_____ ,

_____ _____ __ _____ ,

_____ __ _____

_____ _____ _____ _____ _____

_____ _____ :

_____ , _____ ;

__ , ____ _____ _____

_____ _____ _____

_____ _____

__ _____ _____ _____ ,

___ _____ _____ ,

_____ •

____ _____

_____ _____ _____ •

_____ •

1   Deus

2   Unigenitus cuius per vitam

3   resurrectionem et mortem

4   nobis suam salutis aeternae

5   comparavit praemia

6   quaesumus concede

7 sacratissimo ut mysteria haec

8   Virginis beatae Mariae

9   recolentes Rosario

10   et quod continent imitemur

11   promittunt quod et

12   assequamur

13   eundem Per

14 nostrum Dominum Christum

15   Amen

————,

O God,

———— ———————— ———— ————,

Whose Only-Begotten Son, by His life,

——————— —— ————————,

death and resurrection,

————— ———————— ———— ————,

has for us the rewards of eternal salvation

———————— ———————:

purchased:

————————, ——————————;

grant, we beseech Thee,

——————, ——————— ——————————— ———————

that by these mysteries of the most holy Rosary

———————— ———————— ——————

of the Blessed Virgin Mary,

————————— ————————————

meditating on them,

—— —————————— ———————— ——————————,

we may both imitate what they contain,

—— —————— ———————————,

and what they promise,

————————————·

we may obtain.

————— ——————————

Through the same

———————————— —————————— ——————————·

Christ our Lord.

—————·

Amen.

All Words

nostrum   Amen   eundem

Christum quaesumus;

ut sacratissimo

beatae   haec   recolentes

et   Mariae per   promittunt

assequamur Per salutis nobis

et quod Unigenitus

resurrectionem   suam

continent   et comparavit

concede Deus   cuius

Dominum aeternae   praemia

imitemur vitam mortem

mysteria Virginis

Rosario quod

Deus,

cuius Unigenitus per vitam,

mortem et resurrectionem

suam nobis salutis aeternae

praemia comparavit:

concede, quaesumus;

ut, haec mysteria sacratissimo

beatae Mariae Virginis

Rosario recolentes.

et imitemur quod continent,

et quod promittunt,

assequamur.

Per eundem

Christum Dominum nostrum.

Amen.

REFLECTION

A

A/Ab
From (used with ablative)

Ad
To (used with accusative)

Adveniat
Ad + Venire, to come to, arrive at a place

Advocata
Advocate

Aeternam
Eternal, everlasting

Amen
Truly, surely, verily; from Hebrew

Animas
Souls, spirits

Ascendit
He ascended, went up

Ave
Hail! Be well; a salutation, greeting

B

Benedictus/ benedicta/ benedictum
Blessed, praised, adored; from bene (well) + dicere (to speak)

C

Caelum
Heaven

Carnis
Flesh, the body

Catholicam
Universal, all encompassing, from the Greek καθολικός

Christus
Christ, the Anointed, from the Greek χριστός

Clamamus
From Clamare; to cry out, call complain, shout with a loud voice

Clemens
Mild, forbearing, compassionate, merciful, clement

Communionem
Communion, mutual participation, what a community partakes in

Converte
Turn towards (a command)

Creatorem
The Creator, i.e. God

Credo
I believe in, trust in

Crucifixus
Crucified

D

Da
Give; (from dare, a command)

De
From (preposition)

Debita
Debts, i.e. transgressions, or sins

Debitoribus
From debitor, someone who

owes money, a debtor

Descendit
He descended, went down into

Deus
God

Dextram
Right hand side

Die
Day

Digni
Worthy, fitting, deserving

Dimitte
Let go, forgive, release

Dominus
Lord

Dulcedo
Sweetness (n.)

Dulcis
Sweet (adj.)

E

Eia
Exclamation; indeed! come!

Eas/eius
From is/ea/id, he/she/it

Ecclesiam
Church, an assembly of people

Efficiamur
May we be made (worthy)

Erat
It was; from esse

Ergo
Therefore, on account of this, as a result

Est/es
He is/you are; from esse

Et
And, also, too

Ex
Out from (preposition)

Exsilium
Exile, banishment

Exsules
Exiled people, wanderers, the banished

F

Fiat
Let it be done; from facere

Filius
Son, i.e. Jesus Christ

Flentes
Crying, wailing, weeping

Fructus
Fruit

G

Gementes
Mourning

Genitrix
Mother

Gloria
Glory, praise, honor

Gratia
Grace, favor, esteem

H

Hac/hoc
In this place; from hīc

Haec
These

Hevae
Eve

Hodie
Today

I

Iesus
Jesus

Igne
Fires

Illos
Those

In
In (preposition)

Inde
Thence, from where

Indigent
(They) want for, stand in need of something

Inferiori
Lower, infernal (adj.)

Inferos
Lower regions, Hell

L

Lacrimarum
Of tears

Libera
Free, liberate

M

Malo
Evil

Maria
Mary

Mater
Mother

Maximae
Of the most

Misericordes
Mercy, tender-heartedness, compassion

Mortuus
Death

N

Natus
Born

Ne
Don't

Nomen
Name

Noster
Our

Nunc
Now

O

O
Calling upon someone, getting their attention, O! You!

Oculos
Eyes

Omnes
All

Omnipotentis
All powerful

Ora
Pray

Ostende
Show

P

Panis
Bread

Passus
Suffered

Pater
Father

Peccatoribus
Sinners; from peccator

Peccatorum
Sins; from peccatum

Perduc
Lead

Pia
Pious, devout, kind

Pontio Pilato
Pontius Pilate

Post
After

Praesertim
Especially

Pro
For

Promissionibus
Promises

Q

Quae
Of which

Qui
Who

Quotidianum
Daily

R

℞
Responsum, the response to ℣

Regina
Queen

Regnum
Reign

Remissionem
Foregiveness

Resurrexit
Resurrected

S

Saecula
An age, an indefinitely long time, saecula saeculorum means eternity

Salva
Save

Salve
Hail! A

salutation, greeting

Sanctus
Holy

Sanctorum
Of the Saints

Sanctificetur
May it be made holy

Sed
But

Sedet
He sits

Sepultus
He was entombed

Sicut
Just as

Spes
Hope

Spiritus Sanctus
Holy Spirit

Sub
Under

Suspiramus
We sigh

T

Tu
You

Tecum
With you

Tentationem
Temptation

Terra
Earth

Tertia
The third

U

Unicum
Only

Ut
Like, as, so that

V

℣
Versiculum, a call with an accompanying response, ℞

Valle
Valley

Ventris
Of the womb

Venturus
He will come

Virgo
Virgin

Vita
Life

Vivos
The living

Voluntas
Will, desire, purpose

Need more practice?

Get More Free!

Use the QR code to download the exercises from this book formatted for standard printer paper.

To get more exercises free:

1. *Scan the QR code*
2. *Enter the password OraProNobis*
3. *Click 'download'*
4. *Leave a review on Amazon*
   (*Optional but appreciated*)
5. *Say a rosary for the intentions at the front of this book*
   (*Even more appreciated*)

OUR LADY OF VICTORY, PRAY FOR US

S. DOMINICVS